The Interactive Financial Accounting Lab

Student CD-ROM Manual

Version 2.5

Ralph E. Smith
Arizona State University

Rick Birney
Arizona State University

Irwin
McGraw-Hill

Boston   Burr Ridge, IL   Dubuque, IA   Madison, WI   New York   San Francisco   St. Louis
Bangkok   Bogotá   Caracas   Lisbon   London   Madrid
Mexico City   Milan   New Delhi   Seoul   Singapore   Sydney   Taipei   Toronto

McGraw-Hill Higher Education

A Division of The McGraw·Hill Companies

THE INTERACTIVE FINANCIAL ACCOUNTING LAB:
STUDENT CD-ROM MANUAL

1 2 3 4 5 6 7 8 9 0 IPP/IPP 9 0 9 8 7 6 5 4 3 2 1 0 9

ISBN 0-07-236116-6

http://www.mhhe.com

PREFACE

Welcome to the McGraw-Hill family of interactive accounting courseware. This new and innovative family of products consists of over 40 hours of accounting exercises and feedback and has been designed to assist you in learning this material. No prior computer experience is required to use this courseware.

In this courseware, you are placed in an office environment as if you are working for a company. The office simulation is based on the premise that you are assigned activities by your employer. You are placed in an office environment and assignments are provided on your office calendar. As you proceed through the courseware you are promoted and will receive salary adjustments based on your performance. A fax machine and electronic mail are available for your instructor to communicate to you.

The courseware is structured for you to succeed in the course. After you complete each exercise, you are provided immediate feedback as to the accuracy of your response. If an error is detected in your answer, the courseware will guide you though a four step graded **discovery learning process**.

A convenient review technique is also provided after you have completed an exercise. The review mode provides you with the correct answer, your **first** incorrect answer, and an explanation of the answer.

Introduction

This courseware has been designed to allow you to use it at multiple locations. If you have a computer at home, you can use the CD-ROM provided in this package to load the courseware on your home computer. If you do not have a home computer, you can use the courseware that has been pre-loaded on your school's computer network. Your instructor will provide information on how to access the courseware on the school's computers.

Note: If you do not have a home computer, you will not use the CD-ROM provided in this package. Experience has shown that many students end up purchasing a home computer while using this courseware, so the CD-ROM is provided as a convenience to all students.

This guide is organized into the following chapters:

- *Chapter 1: Installation on Your Home Computer.* This chapter provides instructions for installing the courseware on your home computer.

- *Chapter 2: Using the Courseware.* This chapter is an introduction to the steps involved in using this courseware. These steps apply to both the student home installation or courseware installation on your school's computers.

- *Chapter 3: Using the Courseware at Multiple Locations.* This chapter explains how to activate the multiple location feature of the courseware. This feature allows you to do your courseware lessons at home and at school.

- *Chapter 4: Learning Modules.* This chapter outlines the learning modules that are available in this courseware.

- *Chapter 5: Getting Help.* This chapter discusses the online help system, frequently asked questions as well as a troubleshooting table that may assist you in diagnosing problems.

Provided to you in this package are:
1. The Student Manual you are now reading
2. The courseware CD-ROM

In addition to these items, you may need a **high density formatted disk** if you decide to perform your assignments at both home and at school. This will be discussed later.

Acknowledgments

This manual, and the courseware it supports, are the results of many people's efforts and insights. The process of development and testing has followed the same learning model we think is best for the students -- interactive, cooperative and responsive to feedback.

We appreciate the editorial advice and assistance of the McGraw-Hill staff, particularly Stewart Mattson, Jackie Scruggs, and Irene Baki. Suggestions and comments from users of the software are appreciated.

Ralph E. Smith   Email: **Ralph.Smith@asu.edu**

Rick Birney   Email: **Rick.Birney@asu.edu**

CONTENTS

Chapter 1: Installation on your Home Computer

The courseware is designed so that you can complete your assignments at home or at school. Your instructor already has the courseware installed and will provide instructions on how to access the courseware from the computers at your school. The courseware CD-ROM provided with this package is used to load the courseware on your own personal computer. If you do not have your own computer, the CD-ROM should be saved in a safe location in case you decide to purchase a computer at a later date.

If you do not have a home computer, proceed to chapter two.

The interactive courseware is a Microsoft Windows based application. To use this program, you need

- A 486 or higher based personal computer.
- Microsoft Windows version 3.1 or later.

This courseware also works with Microsoft Windows 95

- A minimum of 8 MB of RAM; however, 16 MB is recommended.
- A 1.44 MB 3.5 inch floppy disk drive.
- 2X CD-ROM drive or better
- Approximately 15 MB of free disk space on your hard disk drive.

Installation of the Courseware

The courseware comes on a CD-ROM. Use the following steps to start the installation:

1. Start up Windows.

2. Insert the CD-ROM into the CD-ROM drive.

3. Choose *Run* from the *File Menu* of the program manager. The *Run* dialog box appears. **Note:** If you are using Windows 95, click on the *Start* button and choose *Run* from the menu.

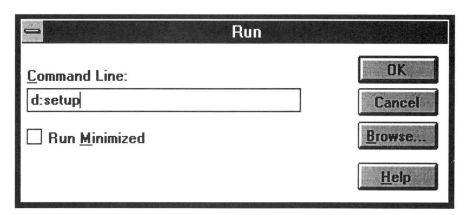

4. Type **d:\setup** (if your CD-ROM is in the D drive) or **f:\setup** (if your CD-ROM is in the F drive) and press *Enter*. The *Courseware Installation* screen appears.

Note: The destination directory in the above figure is denoted as *xxxxxx*. The directory name is usually assigned based on the courseware product that you are using.

5. Ensure that the directory displayed in the *Destination directory* box is the directory where you want to install the program. The installation program assumes that you will be installing the courseware on drive C, the hard drive. If you are using another drive, you may change the destination directory by typing in the new drive letter or directory name. You may also click on the *Browse* button to select the required directory.

6. The three options on the installation screen refer to the following:

   • *Full Install*: Installs all files in the selected directory.
   • *Custom Install*: Ignore this option for now.
   • *Exit*: Allows you to exit the installation program.

   Click on the *Full - Install all files* button to start the installation.

7. The *Courseware Installation* window appears.

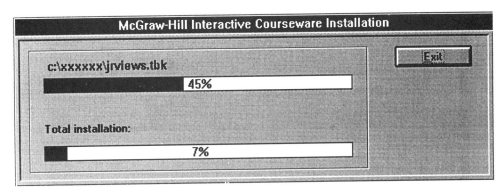

8. When the installation is complete, the question "*Do you want Setup to create Program Manager Groups?*" will appear. Click on *Yes*. This will create a courseware group in the program manager.

9. Next you are informed that the *Installation of the Interactive Courseware is complete*. Click on the *OK* button.

This completes the installation of the courseware. Notice that a new group called **McGraw-Hill Interactive Courseware** has been added to the program manager and it contains an icon. Clicking on this icon will start up the courseware. The figure depicted below displays a generic icon name. The actual icon name is assigned based on the courseware product that you are using.

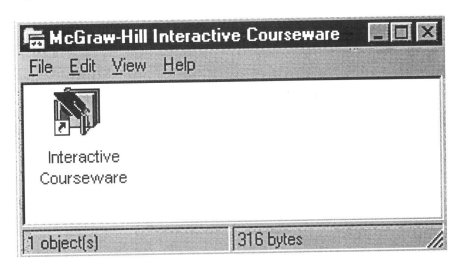

10. You now need to complete the registration card that is included with this manual. Fill in all the details requested on the card. Remember to sign and date the card. Submit the completed registration card to your instructor. Make a note of the software serial number that is printed on the card. You will need the number later when you complete the Employee Registration Card. Ser. No.: _____

Chapter 2: Using the Courseware

This chapter is an introduction to the steps involved in using this courseware. These steps apply to both the student home installation or courseware installation on your school's network computers. Your instructor will provide you with detailed information on how to access the courseware on the school's computer network if this is available.

A. Online Courseware Registration - School Network or Home Version

Follow these directions to start up the courseware for the <u>first</u> time:

1. Double click on the *Interactive Courseware* icon (the actual icon name is assigned based on the courseware product that you are using) in the *McGraw-Hill Interactive Courseware* group in the program manager. **Windows 95 Users:** Click on the *Start* button and select *Programs*. Find and click on the *McGraw-Hill Interactive Courseware* from the list of installed programs. Click on the *Interactive Courseware Name* that appears.

Note: This courseware is not compatible with large system fonts. The courseware checks your computer settings and will inform you if your font size is not compatible. Please refer to the Troubleshooting Table in this manual to correct this problem.

2. The start up screen of the courseware appears. Click on the *Test your Computer* button to perform a courseware compatibility test.

3. Click on the *Enter Building* button to begin.

4. You are asked for your student ID (nine digit social security number) and a password. Enter your social security number and press the *Enter* key.

    The password is a unique combination of letters or numbers that you wish to use in order to restrict access to your data files. Enter your password.

    Click on the *OK* button when you have typed in the ID and password in the boxes provided on the login screen.

5. If you are using the courseware from your home computer, the *First Time User* dialog box will appear. If you are using the courseware on your school's network, the *Employee Account Not Found* dialog box will appear indicating that your Social

Security number and Password was not found in the listing of registered students. Click on the *Register Me* button.

6. The *Employee Information Card* screen should now be displayed. The employee information card must be completed. You and your instructor are the only ones who have access to this information. Notice that the student ID and password have been carried over from the previous screen.

Employee Information Card

A. Employee Information

Software Serial No.:	0897-123		
Social Security Number:	123456789	Employee Access Password:	fun
First Name:	Fred		
Last Name:	Smith		
Address:	123 N. Central Avenue Apt. 24		
City,State,Zip:	Tempe, AZ 85287		
Primary Phone:	602-222-3333 work		
Secondary Phone:	602-222-4444 home		

B. Training Course Information

Section Number:	112233	Instructor:	
Course Name:			

Exit with out saving changes   Save and Exit

7. On the employee information card screen, type in the *software serial number* from the software registration card included with this manual, your *name, address* and *phone number*. Your address and phone number are optional. Your name, address, phone number, and password can be changed during the semester. If you are using the courseware from the school's network computer, type in your instructor supplied *section number*.

8. Click on the *Save & Exit* option when you have finished. A box will appear asking you to enter your social security number. Enter your *Social Security number* and click on the OK button. Next enter your *Password* and click on the OK button.

9. Click on the *Registration Complete* dialog box. This completes the registration process. **NOTE**: You must fill out the Employee Information Screen at each location you will be accessing the courseware. For example, if you will be using the

courseware from both home and school, you must fill out the Employee Information Card at both locations. This will be covered in more details in Chapter 3 - Using the Courseware at Multiple Locations.

The main courseware login screen should now be displayed. Enter your *Social Security Number* and *Password* and click on the OK button.

If you are working at home and have forgotten your password, type in your social security number, and leave the password blank. After three attempts, an Invalid ID and Password window will appear from which you can view your password. For security, if you are working at school and forget your password, you must see your instructor.

B. Office Lobby

After entering a valid Social Security number and Password, the courseware will take you to the Office Lobby screen. The office lobby screen contains four buttons. These buttons perform the following:

Enter Office Button -- Clicking on this button will take you to your desktop.

Employee Information Button -- During the term of the course, you may want to make changes to your employee registration card if you move or you need to change your password. Clicking on this button displays your employee information card.

Review Work Log Button -- Your progress report will appear when you click on this button. The progress report shows for each assignment the date it was completed, a description, your grade, the percent complete, the points assigned by the instructor, and whether the assignment was optional.

The Office Bulletin Board can be accessed from the progress report screen. The Office Bulletin Board shows your current position and salary within the company. Your position and salary changes as you complete each assignment.

Leave Building --Clicking on this button will exit you from the courseware.

Click on the *Enter Office* button. If this is your first time entering your new office you may have a fax message. Read the message and click on the fax *Close* button.

C. The Office

Your office desktop includes a Phone/Fax, Email, Calculator, Notes, Calendar and Reference icons. A real time clock displays the current time and date.

Each of the office icons are explained below:

Reference Book - The reference book contains information related to the activity on which you are currently working. It is available for you to review material while doing a particular exercise. You may access the reference book before starting an exercise. The

REGISTRATION CARD

№ FA 04371

This registration card must be completed and turned in to your instructor or lab administrator before you use the Accounting Courseware.

Name: _____ _____
        Last   *First*

Course Name: _____

Section Number: _____

Term: _____ Year: _____

Professor's Name: _____

This completed card is proof that you have paid the fee for using the Accounting Courseware.

_____
Signature

___/___/___
Date

software is designed to accept both keyboard commands and mouse click commands. For example, to access the reference book, click on the icon, or press the **F5** function key.

Calendar - This icon is used to access your assignments.

Notes - The note pad can be used to write notes to yourself. To access the note pad, click on the icon, or press the **F8** key.

Calculator - The calculator can be accessed by pressing the **F7** key or by clicking on the icon provided. This will result in a calculator being displayed.

Phone/Fax - A message is displayed automatically when your instructor needs to communicate with everyone in the class. To dismiss a fax, click on the fax Close button. A fax that is automatically generated by the simulation is displayed one time. A fax generated by your instructor may be viewed again by clicking on the Phone/Fax icon. A green light on the fax machine indicates that the fax is still available for review.

E-Mail - The word "Mail" will blink on the computer icon whenever an Electronic Mail (E-Mail) message has been sent to you. The E-Mail is used by your instructor to communicate with you directly. To view the current E-Mail messages, click on the *E-Mail* icon. A listing of all active E-Mail messages will be displayed. Highlight the E-Mail message you wish to read and click on the *View Mail* button. To delete an E-Mail message, highlight the E-Mail message to be deleted and click on the *Delete Mail* button.

D. Getting Started

A built-in tutorial has been provided as part of the courseware. You can access this tutorial both at home and at school. The built-in tutorial has three lesson components that are designed to assist you in learning the courseware. Please do not skip these lessons. They are very valuable in helping you learn how to use the courseware. Follow these steps to access the tutorial program:

1. From your *Office*, click on the *Calendar* icon. The calendar displays the lessons that are available in the program. Your instructor will provide instructions as to which lessons need to be completed. The left and right arrow buttons allow you to navigate through the various calendar pages.

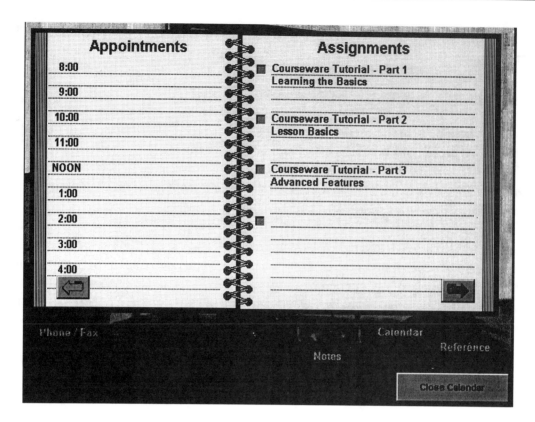

2. Click on the *Courseware Tutorial - Part I* text on the calendar page to launch the first tutorial lesson. The courseware lesson screen will be displayed. At the top of each lesson screen is the Lesson Menu Bar. The lesson menu bar contains functions that assist you in the use of the courseware. The tutorial lessons explain the function of each button.

The calendar button is always used to exit a lesson. When entering and exiting a lesson, the courseware will update your lesson status file. It is important that you always enter and exit the courseware properly to ensure that your lesson status is saved properly.

To exit the courseware properly, click on the *Calendar* button to return to the calendar page, the *Close Calendar* button on the calendar page to return to the Office screen, the *Leave Office* on the office screen to return to the Lobby screen, and then the *Leave Building* button to exit the courseware.

3. Complete the three Courseware Tutorials before attempting to do any of the exercise lessons. Your instructor will tell you what lessons must be completed.

This completes the start up procedure.

Chapter 3: Using the Courseware at Multiple Locations

This courseware is designed to allow you to perform your assignments at multiple locations (school network or home). The courseware will update your student log to the local drive (home) or to the school network if you are working at school. If you perform some of your assignments at home and later decide to complete an assignment at school, a **Student Data Disk** is needed to keep both locations in synchronization. The courseware will update your student log on the local drive (or school network) plus update the student data disk to be used if you change locations. In other words, the student data disk contains lesson information that is used to update your current computer location.

NOTE: The blank student data disk is not provided in your courseware package, you must supply a formatted high density (HD) disk. A student data disk is not needed if the courseware is used at one location only.

It is very important to understand that you must have previously completed the online Employee Information Card screen registration process at both locations (school network or home) before you can activate the multiple location feature.

Multiple Location Activation

To activate the multiple location feature of this courseware, follow these simple instructions:

1. Label a new (formatted) high density (HD) disk as: *Student Data Disk* and write your name and section number on the disk in case it is lost.

2. Access the courseware as normal and click on the *Employee Info.* button on the Office Lobby screen.

3. Click on the *check box* shown below that indicates that you will be using the courseware on both the home computer and the school's network computers.

4. A dialog box will appear cautioning you that a Student Data Disk will be needed for this function. Click on the *OK* button to confirm that you want to activate the multiple location feature.

5. Click on the *Save and Exit* button to indicate that you want to save and exit with this new feature active. Another dialog box will appear indicating that the Home/School Computer Use has been activated. Click on the *OK* button to continue.

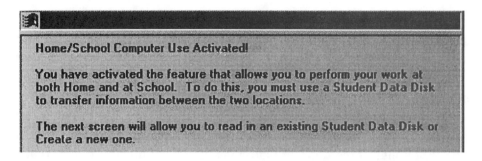

6. The *Student Data Disk Update* screen should now be displayed. The student data disk update screen is used whenever you **enter** or **leave** the program. It provides for a **four step** process to either read (enter) or save to (leave) your student data disk.

Insert a blank high density diskette into your floppy disk drive and click on either the *Drive A* or *Drive B* selection box.

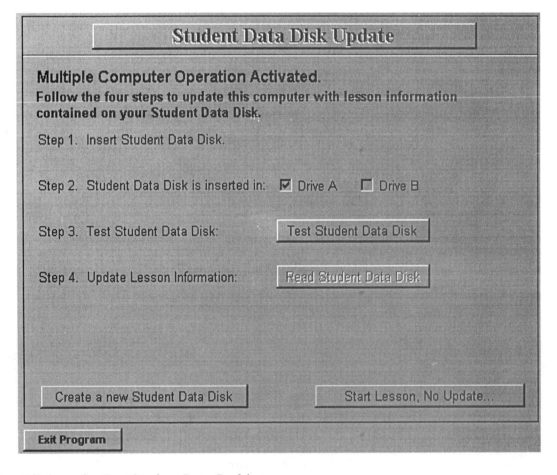

7. Click on the *Test Student Data Disk* button.

8. In the previous step, the Test Student Data Disk button checked to see if your student data disk contained any lesson information. If your student data disk does not contain any information yet, a *Student Data Disk not Found!* dialog box will appear. If you see this dialog box, **proceed to step 9.**

If your student data disk contains lesson information (already activated the multiple locations feature) from another computer, you will see the following:

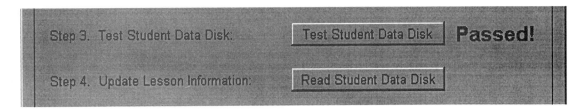

The *Passed!* text indicates that your student data disk contains the necessary lesson information files. Click on the *Read Student Data* Disk button. **Proceed to step 11.**

9. The *Student Data Disk not Found* dialog box is shown below:

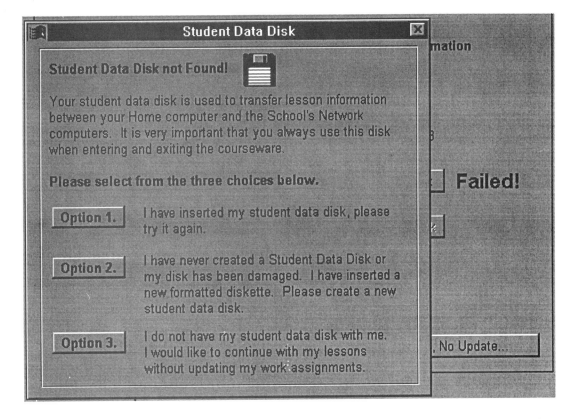

Three options are available in this dialog box. Option 1 allows you to try reading the data disk again. Option 2 creates a new data disk. Option 3 allows you to proceed without using a the data disk. Click on the *Option 2* button to create a new data disk.

10. Click *OK* when prompted by the *Insert a formatted disk* dialog box.

11. An *Information Window* dialog box will appear indicating that the courseware is saving your lesson information.

12. Click on the *OK* button when prompted by the *Student Data Disk has been successfully created* dialog box.

This completes the multiple location activation process.

Note:

1. You must activate the multiple location feature at both your home and school computer locations for this feature to work. If you are unsure whether you have done this, go to the Employee Info. screen and see if the multiple location check box has been checked.

2. Once the multiple location feature is active, you will be required to perform the four step student data disk process whenever you **Enter** and **Exit** the courseware.

Chapter 4: Courseware Learning Modules

The learning modules that are available in this courseware package are outlined below.

Courseware Orientation Tutorials (1,2 and 3)

Introduction to Accounting Equation and Financial Statements

Analyzing Business Transactions

Transactions Analysis: Debit and Credit Rules

Recording Transactions in the General Journal and Posting to the General Ledger

Accrual Basis and Cash Basis Methods of Accounting

Preparing Adjusting Entries

Preparation of a Worksheet and Completion of Accounting Cycle - Service Firm

An Alternative Method of Recording Referrals and Preparing Reversing Entries

Accounting for Merchandising Operation - Perpetual Inventory System

Periodic Inventory System

Subsidiary Ledgers and Special Journals

Inventory Costing Methods

Extension Topics -
    Cash and Receivables
    Investments in Equity Securities
    Operating Assets
    Current Liabilities
    Bonds Payable
    Stockholders' Equity
    Statement of Cash Flows
    Analysis of Financial Statement

Chapter 5: Getting Help

A. Online Help System

The courseware contains an online help system that is available throughout the program. It is intended as a simple refresher of the important material covered in the three tutorial modules. To access the online help system, press the **F1** key.

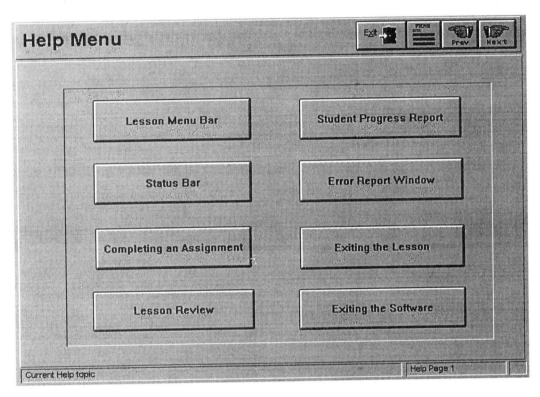

Click on one of the help topic buttons to view that help area. You may exit the online help at any time by clicking on the *Exit* icon.

B. Frequently Asked Questions

Study Questions:

1. Do I need to read my textbook to do well on the courseware?

   Answer: Yes! This courseware has been designed to assist you in learning this material. It is not intended to replace your textbook. Please make sure you read your textbook before attempting the lessons in this courseware.

2. Some of the questions in the lessons were not covered in the Reference Book! Why?

Answer: The Reference Book has been constructed to contain useful information that can assist you in this courseware. It is not the intent of the Reference Book to replace your text. The Reference Book does not contain all the answers!

Operational Questions:

1. I'm confused about the proper punctuation to enter my answers! What do I use?

Answer: Do not enter punctuation or other numeric symbols unless the exercise specifically requests you to do so. For example: commas, $, #, _, -, etc. are not normally used to enter answers.

2. I had the answer right but the #$%$ computer marked it wrong! Why?

Answer: Remember that the REVIEW MODE saves your first answer. It is used when you activate the Review Mode. If you answer an answer field correctly on the 2nd, 3rd or 4th attempt, the Review Mode will still report that you missed that answer field on the first attempt. The correct answer is displayed in the answer field, not your answer. The correct answer Explanation window shows your first answer in red, the correct answer in blue, and an explanation of the answer.

Technical Questions:

1. It seems I am experiencing a lot of General Protection Fault (CRASHES) when using the software! What is wrong?

Answer: If you should encounter a General Protection Fault (GPF) type error when using the courseware, the program will be terminated. Experience has shown that most students try to continue or ignore these problems. This makes things even worse. When you experience a GPF type problem, it is best to EXIT Windows and restart your computer to clear all these types of errors from memory. If you do not do this, continued use of the courseware will most likely cause more errors to occur. This is a problem with Windows and not the courseware.

2. The text on some of the lessons screens seems to be formatted incorrectly. It's hard to read! Why?

Answer: If you find that the text is wrapping incorrectly on your computer screen or it seems that some of the text is missing, your computer display settings may be incompatible with this software. Please check to see that your Windows display settings have been set to 640x480 resolution, 256 Colors and Small Font setting.

3. Every time I enter my Social Security number and Password, I get the message: "The most recent save was interrupted, this book may be corrupted." What do I do?

   Answer: This message indicates that the file that contains your lesson status information was interrupted during a save. To fix this problem, click on the *Ok* button on the error message until you get to the Office Lobby screen. Press the *[F4]* error report function key to access the error reporting function. Click on the *Fix Corrupted File* button and follow the instructions.

4. When I enter a lesson, I get an error message indicating that something is not a number! What do I do?

   Answer: Whenever you enter or leave a lesson, the courseware updates your lesson status file. Sometimes this file gets damaged due to system crashes. If this should happen to you, simply exit the program and re-enter the program. Go to the Review Work Log screen and press the Lesson Integrity button to correct any problems with the lesson status. If this does not fix the problem, ask your instructor for some assistance.

5. The courseware really seems to run slowly. What's wrong?

   Answer: Due to the graphical nature of this courseware and Windows, you should have at least 16MB of RAM in your computer for best results.

C. Troubleshooting Table

PROBLEM	• POSSIBLE SOLUTION
There is not enough memory on your home computer to load the start up program.	• Check your base memory. You must have at least 512K base memory for the install program to work properly. • Remove any memory resident programs (TSRs) in the AUTOEXEC.BAT and CONFIG.SYS files.
Large system font error message. This courseware is NOT compatible with LARGE system fonts.	• Reset the windows system fonts to SMALL fonts before using this courseware. Please refer to your Microsoft Windows documentation (control panel/display) if you are not familiar with how to change this setting.
Text on the exercise screens is not lined up properly.	• Check to make sure you have the arial and courier new true type fonts loaded on your system: • Set your computer display to 640x480 with small fonts. If you are not sure how to do this, ask someone for help. • Check to make sure that you do not have LARGE system fonts selected.
Program does not occupy the full screen.	• Check to make sure your screen resolution is set to 640x480.
Invalid Date or Not a Number Error messages.	• Check your international settings to make sure that they are set to English (United States).
Input/Output Error reading your student data disk.	• Delete the files on your data disk and try saving again. • Replace your student data disk with a new formatted disk.
Review Work Log screen denotes an error when reading your lesson status file.	• Student lesson performance file on the hard disk is damaged. Use the [Lesson Integrity] button on the Work Log screen to fix this problem.
After entering the courseware you constantly see a white error box message that says: "The most recent save was interrupted, this book may be corrupted."	• Student lesson performance file was interrupted during a save operation. Access the [F4] error reporting feature in the courseware. Click on the red [Fix Corrupted File] button and follow the instructions.
Your hard disk does not have enough room for the software and therefore installation is incomplete.	• Delete any old files from your hard disk.